The History of the Bagpipe

First published in 2009 by
Appletree Press Ltd
The Old Potato Station
14 Howard Street South
Belfast BT7 1AP

Tel: +44 (028) 90 24 30 74
Fax: +44 (028) 90 24 67 56
Email: reception@appletree.ie
Web: www.appletree.ie

Copyright © Appletree Press, 2009
Text by Hugh Cheape
Photographs as acknowledged on p96

First published in 2000 as *The Book of the Bagpipe* by Appletree Press

All rights reserved. Printed in China. No part of this publication may be reproduced or transmitted in any form or by any means, electronic, photocopying, recording or in any information and retrieval system, without prior permission in writing from the publisher.

A catalogue record for this book is available from the British Library.

The History of the Bagpipe

ISBN-13: 978 1 84758 135 8

Desk and Marketing Editor: Jean Brown
Copy-editor: Jim Black
Designer: Stuart Wilkinson
Production Manager: Paul McAvoy

9 8 7 6 5 4 3 2 1

AP3619

The History of the Bagpipe

Hugh Cheape

Pipe Major William Ross (1823–1891) in the portrait by Kenneth MacLeay for Queen Victoria in 1866.

Contents

Introduction	7
The Pipes of Scotland	9
An Ancient Tradition	17
Material Evidence	26
Europe and the 12th-Century Renaissance	40
From England to Scotland	50
The Music of the Folk	55
Burgh Pipers	68
The Highland Bagpipe	78
Siubhal	89
Further Reading	94
Acknowledgements	95

The Piper to the Laird of Grant, William Cumming, painted by Richard Waitt in 1714. This striking and important image symbolises the musical and social context of the bagpipe in Gaelic Scotland.

Introduction

Scotland has a wealth and variety of music and one of the oldest and most successful of wind instruments – the bagpipe. In essence, the bagpipe is a wind instrument with melody pipe or 'chanter' on which the music is played and with fixed note 'drone' or 'drones'. It is a reed instrument like the oboe and clarinet; a small blade or pair of blades made of seasoned cane, bound onto a 'staple' or copper tube and inserted into the end of the pipe, vibrates under air pressure to produce the sound.

The best known and most widely recognised is Scotland's Highland bagpipe – in Gaelic, *a' Phìob* or *Pìob Mhór* – although in terms of a probably world-wide history and evolution of the bagpipe, this represents a relatively recent stage. It is almost impossible now to document the origins of the Highland bagpipe apart from suggesting that it derived from European types of bagpipe and was probably being played in an early form towards the north and western parts of Scotland from the 15th century.

What we have today owes more to the intervening centuries and to the history of Gaelic Scotland;

the instrument with its robust sound and rare tonal qualities is the creation of the society of the historical *Gàidhealtachd* which has contributed so much to the musical wealth of Scotland. It is a matter of celebration that the bagpipe today is the vehicle of a lively and thriving, even explosive, musical tradition.

The Pipes of Scotland

In different forms, the bagpipe has been played in Scotland probably for most of 600 years. The best known instrument, at least over the last 100 years, has been the 'Great Highland Pipe' or *Piob Mhór*, thus qualified to distinguish it from other and smaller bagpipes played in Scotland. The evidence of music, history and art suggests that there has been an almost bewildering variety of types of pipes played in Scotland.

As late as the middle of the 19th century, the bagpipe maker, Alexander Glen of Edinburgh, was advertising six different types of Highland bagpipe alone. There were few rules or standards for making bagpipes and makers presumably made their instruments to achieve a sound which suited them or the player. From the historical record, which is not in any sense complete, it is difficult to detect professional bagpipe makers before the 18th century. In so far as they were trained craftsmen, it was probably more often as wood turners, and this helps to explain the variety of pitch of surviving old instruments and the distinctive 'modal' scale of the bagpipe which tends to defy definition in classical terms. The power and musicality of the instrument must

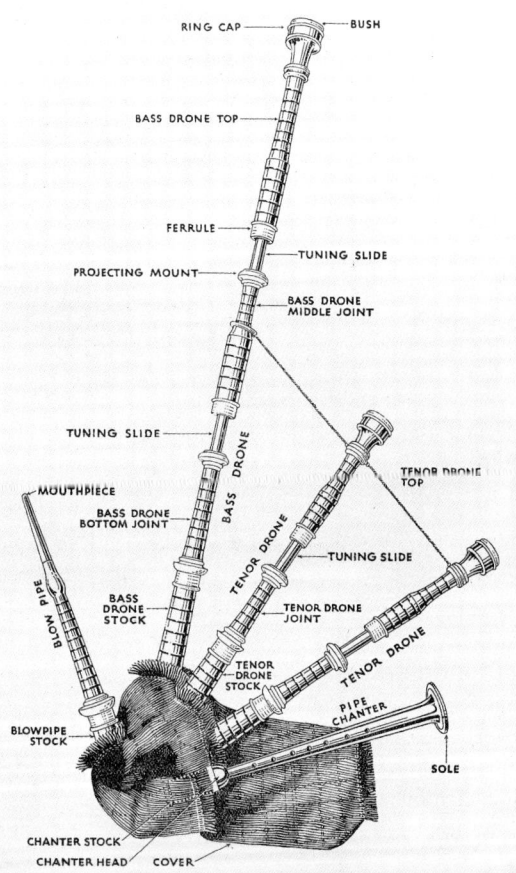

Diagram of the Highland bagpipe showing the separate sections with traditional technical terms as applied by the reputable bagpipe maker Peter Henderson (1851-1903) of Glasgow in his catalogue, first published in Peter Henderson Ltd., *Catalogue of Bagpipes* (etc.) Glasgow.

now be beyond dispute, and similarly it can be claimed that the Highland bagpipe of today, well-made and well-played, is an impressive musical instrument.

In the Highland bagpipe and similar instruments, the air pressure comes from a bag of skin (or often today of a synthetic material), inflated from the player's mouth through a blowpipe and held against the body and pressed under the arm. The distinctive and memorable sound of the pipes is at least partly due to the use of the bag as a reservoir of air to maintain a constant air pressure on the reeds. The art of piping is to produce an even tone and avoid any rise and fall in sound or pauses between notes. The three drones of the Great Highland bagpipe – bass drone and two tenor drones, each with its own reed – sound a continuous fixed note to accompany the melody. Before inflating the bagpipe, all the reeds, including chanter and drones, can be adjusted for strength and tuning by lowering or raising them in their 'seats' or by constricting or widening the airflow, both of which sets of alteration will respectively sharpen or flatten the tone. The drones must be carefully tuned to the chanter and to each other, and this is done as the prelude to playing by adjusting the lengths of each drone which is made up of two or three separate joints.

The melody is played on the chanter, pierced with finger holes and played with both hands. The musical range of the chanter is limited because it only has nine notes, but, with changes in fashion and interest in the past, the scale of some bagpipes was extended by the addition of keys to the chanter, as in the case of the Irish *uileann* pipes and the Northumbrian smallpipes. Much musical performance is characterised by more or less emphatic sound and pauses or small intermittent silences, none of which is acceptable on the Scottish pipes. Character is given to the even flow of sound by strict timing to produce distinctive rhythms and gracenoting to ornament and separate the notes. Gracenotes, as rapid short notes or elaborate combinations of short notes inserted between the notes of the melody, give the native musical idiom of Scotland much of its strength and distinctiveness.

The bagpipe exists for the music played on it and wherever the bagpipe is played, repertoires consist of music for dancing, music for singing, and music for listening to, such as instrumental versions of songs. The history of this music in

The Pipes of Scotland

the longer term is difficult to determine because it was rarely written down, but it is not without significance that Scotland has one of the richest folk music traditions in the world. Good music is never the preserve of any one instrument or medium and will readily transfer between them. This has always suited the piping tradition of Scotland which has depended on learning and transmitting music by word of mouth. This persists in the rich Gaelic traditions of *port-a-bial*

Set of French bellows-blown pipes or *musette* which was said to belong to Prince Charles Edward Stewart – 'Bonnie Prince Charlie'.

or 'mouth music' and *canntaireachd* or 'chanting' in which a unique word notation corresponds in systematic method to the intricacies of the music to be played and could be used to teach and transmit it. Traditional musicians, such as fiddlers and pipers, did not read or write down their music and little is known about it in detail until the 18th century when collectors such as Allan Ramsay and Robert Burns began to record first the words and then the music of songs. The bagpipe especially was late in using staff notation and Scottish pipe music was not systematically handled until the first half of the 19th century. As traditional music was written down, arranged and published, the swirling pool of folk music began to crystallise and become less fluid. Ancient music had survived in a process of re-using and re-naming inherited or half-heard old melodies so that what might be national anthems in one culture, would be 'jingles' and nursery rhymes in another. The melody of 'Jenny's Bawbee' in Scotland is the English 'Polly put the kettle on', and the probably ancient 'Kafoozalum' is the Scottish strain of 'Katie Bairdie' or 'Sheriffmuir'. Claims to the ownership of tunes meant less in the past; the Irish traditional air 'Limerick's Lamentation' is known in Scotland as 'Lochaber no more', a Victorian re-naming of the older native air *Crodh Chailein* or 'Colin's Cattle', a typical Gaelic song which was said to have been learnt from the Good Folk or Fairies. If it ever had to be explained or rationalised, the supernatural would always be a way of appreciating and understanding the perceptible and steady wind of traditional music blowing down through the centuries.

In the Highland bagpipe tradition, song and dance music, as well as marching music, is described in a special sense as 'light music', or *ceòl beag* in Scottish Gaelic; this means literally 'small music' and distinguishes it from *ceòl mór* or 'great music' which is considered as a form of classical music for the Great Highland bagpipe. This is now referred to also as *piobaireachd*, literally and simply meaning 'piping' in Scottish Gaelic – a word which has passed into the English form 'pibroch'. *Piobaireachd* is therefore a generalising term for a particular class of pipe tunes in extended and complex form, dating mainly from the 17th and 18th centuries and commemorating clan gatherings and battles. As music to listen to, it includes salutes to clan chieftains and laments on the deaths of the leading folk of kin and clan and, for the listeners, was powerful in meaning and message. The different tunes as salutes, laments, marches and gatherings were distinguishable by subtleties of melody and rhythm as well as by their words.

Many of the tunes are significantly named, as for example the selection of tunes commemorating the notable clan chieftain, Sir Ruairi Mór MacLeod, who died in 1626 and whose example was thus kept prominently before his people and his own successors, and many of the tunes were originally songs to which there were words. In the 19th and 20th centuries, due to cataclysmic changes suffered by Gaelic society, the songs and tunes tended to become divorced from one another and the latter to become stylised in interpretation and performance in a way that has in many cases been detrimental to them as music. Thus a beautiful old *ceòl mór* pipe tune known in English as 'MacCrimmon's Sweetheart', which may well have been the melody of a song, has lost its words and relies on tradition to explain the very different Gaelic title of Maol Donn as a song in commemoration of a favourite cow which has been stuck perilously and probably fatally in a peat bog.

An Ancient Tradition

In its origins, as far as these can be traced or understood because they are now remote, the bagpipe was never the property of one people or one nation but was a universal musical instrument. This powerful instrument has a long pedigree and derives from earlier and prehistoric reeded pipes such as 'shawms' and 'hornpipes', known and played in Near Eastern and Egyptian civilisations from before about 2,500 BC. These are the names conventionally given to the first pipes; the shawm was usually a turned wooden wind instrument with a double reed and a sound tube in the form of a long narrow cone opening out from top to bottom. It was once widely played in Asia and Europe and survives today, for example, in the vigorous and strident *bombarde* of Brittany. The hornpipe, with a cylindrical bore in the sound tube, could more easily be made of other materials such as metal or bone. It was certainly played in medieval Scotland and, with a bell end formed from a cow's horn, was known to tradition as the 'stock and horn'. The oldest form of definable hornpipe was the *aulos*, given a Greek name but traditionally originating in Phrygia or Asia Minor. As such it associated itself with Hellenistic civilisation and was well known in Rome by the 1st and 2nd centuries AD where it was the instrument of street musicians. With the reeds held directly in the mouth, it had two chanters and when such instruments appear in later sources, they are usually played with the addition of a bag. This is well depicted on a carved bench-end in the 'Cathedral of the Moors' at Altarnun in Cornwall.

Bagpipe with two separate chanters of hornpipe type, 16th century, on a carved bench-end in the 'Cathedral of the Moors' at Altarnun, Cornwall.

An Ancient Tradition

Bags were added to pipes such as these to help blowing, probably as early as Roman times. Although this seems to provide a more convenient and comfortable method of blowing, the bag was not necessarily adopted and shawms continued to be played without a bag and with the reed in the player's mouth. This indicates that early reed instruments could have been played in a bagpipe style with the reed in the mouth but with a constant flow of music maintained by 'circular breathing', that is, maintaining the air pressure in the pipe with the cheeks while taking breaths through the nose. This technique referred to as 'sook 'n blaw' is still used in Scotland for playing the practice chanter.

As a bagpipe with drone accompaniment, it seemed to become a common musical instrument in Europe from the 12th century, itself significantly a renaissance period of relative economic wellbeing. Though it has been widely played in many forms in Europe and Asia throughout history, today the bagpipe or, more obviously, its sound is strongly identified with Scotland, especially in the form of the Highland Bagpipe, and in this form has been exported to many parts of the world and adopted or adapted in sometimes very different cultural

Wooden statuette of a piper playing the *biniou* or traditional small bagpipe of Brittany.

milieux. A distinctive example nearer home is the *cornemuse* or *grand biniou* in Brittany where a culture with its own piping tradition adopted the Highland bagpipe and some of its music and techniques. This added a significant dimension to what was at the time perceived as a declining tradition, the *bombarde* and *biniou* or small pipe as the *jeu de couple* playing in concert at social gatherings and community festivals and especially in the Breton summer religious festivals and pilgrimages – *les Pardons*. The Highland bagpipe was said to have been introduced to Brittany by Gildas Jaffrenou about 1932 to strengthen piping in the face of the popular accordion and a cultural nationalism which did not value Breton traditional life. The creation of a Pipers' Association in 1942, the *Bodadeg ar Sonerion*, laid the foundations of a powerful revival.

It is difficult to produce a credible and brief definition of the Highland bagpipe and its origins within a short compass beyond a few sweeping generalisations. The object begs the questions, 'When was the bagpipe invented?' 'Where was it invented?' 'Who invented it?' Our imagination looks perhaps for a skilful and cunning Highlander musician of medieval times. The notion of an identifiable individual located in time and space has been a conceit encouraged in Scotland and within the Highland piping tradition itself. The notable Gaelic scholar, Rev Dr Norman MacLeod, wrote and published books and periodicals in the early 19th century to provide useful and informative prose for a Gaelic readership. In 1841, he wrote an account in Gaelic, supposedly from traditional material, of the well-known

Drawing of 'Breton Folk' by the English artist, Randolph Caldecott, in the 1870s. The *biniou* and *bombarde* are playing in concert for the *Gavotte*, the best known of the old Breton *rondes* or 'round dances'.

piping family of the MacCrimmons of Skye and included the statement:

> 'The first of his name came from a town in Italy called Cremona; he was a harper, a renowned musician in his own day and generation. He took the name of his birthplace and those who descended from him they called MacCrimmon.'

The origins of the MacCrimmon master pipers and their art in Italy seem to have supplied a straightforward and popular explanation of an otherwise intriguing and mysterious story; it seemed to satisfy our curiosity even though it defied the logic of known history. However, both their name of 'MacCrimmon' and the Gaelic pedigree implicit in this name located them firmly in the medieval culture province of the *Gàidhealtachd* of Ireland and Scotland.

Many writers have discoursed on the origins of the bagpipe both in Scotland and elsewhere in the world but the topic has until recently received very uneven and disappointing treatment from historians, many of whom have depended on mythologies of Scottish history and theories of progressive development from remote origins in

MacCrimmon piper, as a member of the *luch-taighe* or clan chieftain's retinue, playing a salute to his chief, MacLeod of Dunvegan, in an imaginary construction of the 1840s.

An Ancient Tradition

reed-pipes of ancient civilisations. But the pursuit of origins, as we have seen, does not serve to explain and indeed may descend into fallacy. Because of the unevenness of the evidence, such analyses usually present too systematic an account of the past, or start with a set of assumptions and select facts to fit. The example of the MacCrimmons depends on persuading us that we may learn of the origins of the Highland bagpipe by tracing the supposed origins of the family whose reputed pre-eminence gave us the art of piping as it has descended to us today. Research into the origins of the MacCrimmons tells us something about the character of a culture province which stretched from the Butt of Lewis to Cape Clear in the medieval period but little about the origins of Highland piping. For this we have to look elsewhere.

Material Evidence

Besides traditional and written evidence, we have a very incomplete picture of the history of the bagpipe due also to the fragmentary and we assume only partial survival of material. Archaeology, which might be expected to have recovered some early evidence to give us some ideas of typologies and insights into music making, has recovered very little. Woodwind instruments, by their very nature, rarely survive either above or below the ground. Examples seem isolated, such as the metal double-pipe excavated in the Sumerian royal cemetery at Ur of the Chaldees in Mesopotamia, which gives us an initial benchmark of wind instrument origins in the Near East about 2,500–2,800 BC.

The sources have little or nothing to tell us of the bagpipe or piping in Europe between Roman times and about the 12th century. Written evidence of any kind is in poor supply, and only wars and the affairs of church and state merit mention in the annals and chronicles of the day; the pipes as a folk instrument fell below the level of the significant. The pipes of Pictland therefore are exceptional. Stone carvings showing musicians and musical instruments survive in those parts of north and east Scotland known to have been occupied by the Picts, a vigorous people whose remarkable culture brings light to the so-called 'dark ages' before the millennium. Large sculptured stone monuments show harpers and harps, for example, of a type called *cruit* strongly characteristic of Gaelic culture in later centuries. A type of triple-pipe is shown on sculptured stones of the 8th and 9th centuries at Lethendy and Ardchattan and on St Martin's Cross. It also appears in Ireland on the 10th-century St Muireadach's Cross at Monasterboice and on the Cross of the Scriptures at Clonmacnoise. This instrument usually consists of two short pipes, probably chanters, and one long pipe, possibly a drone, played in the hands of one player who appears to have the reeds in his mouth. Information on this instrument and its technical performance is available in the analogous triple-pipe still played in Sardinia and called *launeddas*.

Rare examples of wind instruments have in recent years been recovered from the sea where they have survived in a waterlogged state. A wooden instrument which appears to be a section, approximately 20 cm long, of the melody pipe from a hornpipe or bagpipe is included in the displays in the Roskilde Viking Ship Museum in Denmark, and a 'whistle' was discovered in the hull of the 16th-century *Mary Rose;* the latter was probably a pipe played one-handed with the tabor, traditionally a popular combination with strolling minstrels. Wind instruments in materials other than wood were of course made and examples have been found in Scotland. An excavation in North Berwick in 1907 turned up a brass whistle which is now in the collections of the National Museums of Scotland. It is 14 cm long with six fingerholes – what would today be called a 'penny whistle' – stratified in the earth with pottery of the 14th and 15th centuries. Musical instruments have been customarily made from bone and ivory and the Latin word *tibia* for the shinbone also meant a pipe or flute in classical sources. The larger shinbone would be ideal material for forming a hornpipe chanter with more or less cylindrical bore, and what is undoubtedly a prehistoric tradition was still detectable in the 'stock and horn' of 18th-century Scotland. On the 19th November 1794, Robert Burns wrote to George Thomson with whom he was collaborating over the collection of *Select Scottish Airs*:

'I have, at last, gotten one, but it is a very rude instrument. It is composed of three

Material Evidence

parts: the stock, which is the hinder thighbone of a sheep, such as you see in a mutton ham: the horn, which is a highland cow's horn, cut off at the smaller end, until the aperture be large enough to admit the "stock" to be pushed through the horn, until it be held by the thicker or hip-end of the thigh-bone: and lastly an oaten reed exactly cut and notched like that which you see

Pipe and tabor player typically providing music for dancing. From the title-page of a pamphlet of 1600 'Kemp's Nine Daies Wonder. Performed in a Dance from London to Norwich.'

every shepherd-boy have, when the corn-stems are green and full-grown. The reed is not made fast in the bone, but is held in the lips, and plays loose in the smaller end of the "stock", while the "stock" and horn hanging on its larger end, is held by the hands playing. The stock has six or seven ventiges in the upper side, and one back ventige, like the common flute. This one of mine was made by a man from the Braes of Athole, and is exactly what the shepherds were wont to use in that country. However either it is not quite properly bored in the holes or else we have not the art of blowing it rightly, for we can make little of it.'

The old shepherd's pipe was clearly a rarity by Burns' day but, given the Poet's intense interest in traditional music, he even adopted it as an emblem in a coat-of-arms which he designed for himself. After his death in 1796, his example of the shepherd's pipe was given by Jean Armour, his widow, to a neighbour in Dumfries and is now in the collections of the National Museums of Scotland.

Deprived of early material evidence for the British Isles as a whole, the discovery of fragments of a

Shepherd playing the 'Stock and Horn' in an illustration by the Scottish artist, David Allan (1744-1796) for Allan Ramsay's *Gentle Shepherd*, published in 1788

bagpipe-type instrument at the medieval moated site of Weoley Castle in Warwickshire dated to the late 13th or 14th century has so far been unsurpassed. This is a wooden tube, probably of boxwood, 30 cm long with a cylindrical bore and with one end expanding in a style recognisable from early iconographic representations of bagpipes with a drone; this end is trimmed as for a bone or horn ring-mount, now missing, but precisely comparable with the treatment of the drone tops of sets of pipes to this day.

Most sets of bagpipes consist of up to a dozen and more separate pieces or 'joints' which makes it less likely that old bagpipes survive in their entirety. As a mouth-blown wind instrument, the bagpipe dries out if it is not being played and begins to fall apart; the joints may be damaged or broken and the instrument rapidly becomes unplayable. Players were sometimes at pains to keep their bagpipes going and would go to great lengths to repair and bind up cracks and breakages. But there would also be a tendency to discard broken instruments because their musicality would have deteriorated. There would be little reason to keep these and the consequence is that we have such fragmentary evidence for the bagpipe of past centuries. Some discarded joints from 17th- and early 18th-century instruments survived in the shop of J & R Glen in Edinburgh and are now in the collections of the National Museums of Scotland. What characterised this material was its variety and obvious lack of standardisation so that, for example, of the many pieces of drone surviving from earlier times, it was very difficult to match items which might have come from the same instrument.

Early written evidence is frequently cited to define and explain origins but key terms in early sources may be ambiguous and misleading. Scholars seem to agree that the earliest reference to a bagpipe is in a possibly satirical jibe by the Athenian poet, Aristophanes, of about 425 BC. He describes pipers from Thebes – whom as traditional enemies of Athens he could readily insult – blowing on a pipe with a bag of dogskin and with a chanter of bone. The Emperor Nero has variously been described as fiddling or piping while Rome burned although we shall probably never know which. The Latin author, Suetonius, described the Emperor as being a player of the *tibia utricularius* which has been generally interpreted as a pipe with a skin bag attached. Biblical references to the bagpipe are by no

Piper playing a bagpipe with a single drone, carved on a panel reputed to be from Threave Castle, Galloway, late 15th century. He is one of a series of figures on the panels suggesting a band of travelling players.

means clear since Latin terms were introduced sometimes arbitrarily to serve as the equivalents of words in Hebrew. In Isaiah chapter 5, we read in verse 12 that 'the harp and pipe are in their feasts' but this is more literary artifice than historical evidence. Medieval references, often in neo-Latin such as *utricularis* or *calamis* which have been identified with wind instruments such as bagpipes, cannot necessarily be identified with the certainty implicit in present-day accounts.

Archaeological and iconographic evidence is wonderfully combined in the surviving decoration of some medieval churches. Strong visual imagery is a consistent and important element in medieval art and sculpture, and the bagpipe is found symbolically being played by pigs and angels. There are intriguingly different ways of explaining the pig pipers of the medieval period. On the one hand, by giving the bagpipe to a pig, it emphatically lowers the status of the instrument but associates it with the animal which could provide an airtight reservoir for the pipe bag. On the other hand, it was said that pigs were lovers of music and were often shown in art as musicians, especially in 'Bestiaries' which were a popular type of book in the medieval period describing animals in a sort of 'natural history' but placing them in an 'unnatural history' of allegorical narrative. The decoration of manuscripts with drawings and colour was becoming common practice by the late 13th century. The bagpipe is frequently seen in 'manuscript illumination' in the grip both of humans and of animals. The scribe or artist is often giving us a parody of real life, and animals which were associated with the lower passions of lust and avarice, and therefore with Satan, were offered as visual precept and distraction towards higher passions. The bagpipe has always aroused people's passions to a high degree and were therefore traditionally frowned on by the church.

But this was a good processional instrument and customarily participated in church festivals. It is evident from different parts of medieval Britain and Europe that pipers played for Feast of the Nativity festivals around Christmas, for the Ceremony of the Palms on Palm Sunday, and of course for the Feast of Fools on Twelfth Night. They were popular for providing music on pilgrimage as the accounts of Scottish royal pilgrimages show. James IV went on pilgrimage to the shrines of St Duthac at Tain and St Ninian at Whithorn and paid pipers for entertaining him. A manuscript edition of Chaucer's 'Canterbury

Tales' shows 'Robin with the Bagpype', as a piper pilgrim playing on horseback. This occurs in the text at the description of the Miller, a 'stout carle', and concludes with:

> 'A baggepipe well coude he blowe and sowne,
> And therewith he brought us out of town.'

Apart from manuscript illumination, strong visual imagery may be sculptural detail within the architecture of the building itself, for example on the capitals of columns and eaves decoration, or carvings in the wood of pew ends and misericords, or in stained glass; biblical, spiritual and allegorical stories painted onto glass in the medieval period often included musical instruments and appropriately they are represented as being played by angels. The instruments shown are those which were in use by court musicians and by companies of minstrels at the time when the windows were made. They might be used to illustrate the instruments of King Nebuchadnezzar's orchestra as described in the Book of Daniel; these included 'cornet, flute, harp, sackbut, psaltery, dulcimer and all kinds of music'. Others are found in the psalms as in Psalm 150 in which we are exhorted to praise

Player or minstrel with a droneless bagpipe or *chorus*, dancing and singing, drawn on an English manuscript of the early 14th century.

God with musical instruments such as trumpet, psaltery, harp, timbrel, stringed instruments and organs; the specific names assigned to Hebrew terms may be imprecise, illusory or contradictory, having been filtered through two languages and very different cultures. A sculpted frieze in St Mary's Church in Adderbury, Oxfordshire, translates the spirit of Psalm 150 into stone and shows minstrels offering 'universal praise' to the

Creator through successive orders of music; church music is represented by the portative organ, being sounded by bellows worked with the player's left hand, a device later applied commonly to bagpipes. The musical instruments of the dance are timbrel, bagpipes, symphony and rebec. Military or marching music is represented with trumpets and different species of drums. Minstrelsy itself is represented by the plucked-string psaltery and the harp, then recognised as instruments customarily used to accompany the human voice.

Europe and the 12th-Century Renaissance

The 12th century has been characterised as a period of 'renaissance' in European history when the arts, science and literature flourished in a way in which they had clearly not in the preceding centuries. Identifiable phenomena such as the growth of towns (abundantly clear also in the evidence for 12th-century Scotland and the reign of David I for example), the Crusading movement and the collision and exchange with Islam provided fertile ground for the spread of music and song. The years from 1099 to about 1291 experienced a complex of social, economic and cultural interaction between Muslims and Crusaders, and new instruments of science and music were imported into Europe from the richer cultures of the Middle East. In this period the bagpipe seems to have travelled fast and far and to have developed into the universal musical instrument of medieval Europe. Its presence in a vigorous folk tradition in Eastern Europe is as likely to be attributed to the same renaissance as breathed life into it in Western Europe. Poland, Czechoslovakia, Ukraine, Yugoslavia, Romania, Bulgaria and Macedonia all have remarkable bagpipes with their own histories. Some have suffered varying fortunes, for example, the bagpipe with goat-headed chanter of Hungary had retreated into the hills and had all but disappeared by the end of the 19th century. It was rescued by the folklore- and folkmusic-collecting activity and by the musical genius of Béla Bartók (1881–1945) and Zoltan Kodály (1882–1967). By contrast, it had remained a flourishing tradition for feasts and weddings in Bulgaria where it was always said that 'a wedding without a bagpipe is like a funeral'. The earliest music with which we are in any way familiar because of the possibilities of it still being performed today also belongs to the 12th century when, as we have seen, representations of the bagpipe and pipers begin to proliferate in the surviving illuminated manuscripts and the adornment of church buildings.

The pipes appear in English sources in the 13th century and slightly later in Scotland, the evidence suggesting some form of cultural diffusion northwards and across the sea from Continental Europe and the new towns of Northern France and Flanders. The instrument itself may have been a droneless bagpipe, known from medieval sources as the *chorus*,

French piper playing for a local festival in Central France, early 20th century. His instrument, the *chabrette*, has chanter (*chalumeau*) and a small drone (*petit bourdon*) fixed together in the same stock.

or a bagpipe with drone or drones. Beside the 'chanter' or melody pipe with its series of holes stopped by the fingers to play the tune, the drone sounding a fixed note with its degrees of harmonic tension is a distinguishing characteristic of the bagpipe, extending significantly the levels and volume of sound at the command of the one player and the glory of the instrument. Perhaps the nearest surviving relation of this medieval bagpipe is the *gaita* of North West Spain which thrives in style with many pipe bands and virtuoso performance. The Spanish *gaita* has the wide conical chanter and bass drone with prominent bell-ends which might have stepped out of a medieval manuscript. We know that the bagpipe was then in the hands mainly of itinerant musicians and professional minstrels, a class or caste with a popular following in the medieval period but stigmatized because they were considered capable of destabilising the rigid social order of feudal Europe. These folk on the move were popular because they brought news and gossip, but their lifestyle and morals earned disapproval and their information was seen by those in authority as subversive. Good or bad, minstrels were the formers and informers of popular culture and carried the bagpipe and its music round Europe.

The figure of a professional minstrel or troubadour carved on the ivory stock of a crossbow, about 1450. His bagpipe with a conical chanter and bass drone is a type of instrument represented today by the *gaita* or bagpipe of Galicia and the north-west region of Spain.

Some church music is known from the 12th century although the notation is imprecise and seems to represent aide-mémoire rather than musical score; with this as source material, the reconstruction of melodies may not necessarily be accurate. Music for secular purposes and everyday performance is largely unknown although suggestions may be made. It was a consistent tradition that a popular melody called 'Hey Tutty Tatty' was the music to which Bruce's army marched to Bannockburn and seems to mimic the beating of the drum. It was also known as 'Hey now the day dawis' of which Robert Burns wrote: 'I have met the tradition universally over Scotland, and particularly about Stirling, in the neighbourhood of the scene, that this air was Robert Bruce's March at the Battle of Bannockburn, which was fought in 1314'. Burns commemorated this by writing his anthem of 'Scots wha hae wi' Wallace bled' to the tune; it is still played also as a popular pipe reel called 'The Wind that shakes the Barley'.

Early music forms in Scotland may be inferred from ballad metre, interpolating perhaps with melodies surviving from later medieval sources, and from surviving Eastern European and Near Eastern musical styles; here one may still hear

Volinka

Bagpipe with chanter and bass drone and with bag of undressed goatskin which was seen by the antiquarian, Matthew Guthri, among Finns living in Russia in the late 18th century.

pieces of music of no fixed structure or length where each player has their own stock of motifs which they repeat and combine in various ways throughout a performance, building them into a variety of two- or four-bar phrases. Gracenotes and 'cuttings' are used to separate notes and to ornament the melody. The 'hornpipe' is the name given on the one hand to a type of early musical instrument and on the other to a lively dance tune used by pipers. One or two early hornpipe melodies surviving in the Scottish repertoire in the 18th century may well be pieces of music of this sort; an example may be the short and apparently fragmentary 'Wee Totum Fogg' the surviving words of which, sounding like a mnemonic, are:

> 'Wee Totum Fogg
> Sits upon a creepie,
> Half an ell of grey
> Wad be his coat and breekie.'

Another, typically, taken up by Robert Burns about 1792 and published in *The Scots Musical Museum* with his own verses added to a traditional chorus is 'Hey ca' through', possibly echoing early medieval ring or line dance music or music intended to accompany and lighten the burden of work tasks:

> 'We hae tales to tell,
> And we hae sangs to sing;
> We hae pennies to spend,
> And we hae pints to bring.
>
> Hey ca' thro', ca' thro'
> For we hae muckle ado,
> Hey ca' thro', ca' thro'
> For we hae muckle ado'.

The poem attributed to James I (r.1406–1437), 'Peblis to the Play', mentions not only the pipes but also significantly their social milieu in the context of an archaic and prehistoric dance:

> 'With that, Will Swane cam sueitand out
> Ane meikle miller man;
> Gif I sall dance, have done, lat se,
> Blaw up the bagpipe than,
> The salmon's dance I mon begin.'

Ballads too may preserve early instrumental melodies. The classic narrative *oran mór* or 'muckle sang' has survived strongly in Scotland from a remote time and of unknown authorship, and doubtless tells us something of early bagpipe music of the 12th and later centuries. A song that Robert Burns described as an ancient survivor from his own native Ayrshire was 'Johnny Faa the Gypsy Laddie' or 'The Ballad of Johnny Faa'. He recorded it for the published collection of *The Scots Musical Museum*. The tune is still played on the Highland bagpipe as 'The Bonnie Hoose o' Airlie' and is the same as a tune scripted for lute in the early 17th-century Skene Manuscript where it is called 'Lady Cassillis' Lilt'. The words are classic ballad:

> 'The gypsies came to our Lord's yett,
> And vow but they sang sweetly;
> They sang sae sweet, and sae compleat,
> That down came the fair lady.'

From England to Scotland

Many of our earliest impressions of bagpipes in the British Isles come from carvings in stone and wood in church buildings. The great churches in Gloucester, Tewkesbury, Cirencester, Ripon and Exeter for example are rich in carvings of musical instruments. Decorative sculpture including pipes and pipers is particularly prominent in English architecture of the 14th century and this is remarkably well represented in the surviving work in Exeter Cathedral. The Cathedral was dedicated to the Blessed Virgin Mary and to St Peter, and the coronation and enthronement of the Mother of Christ is the centrepiece of the decorative scheme. Angelic choirs and minstrels are here seen as the special attendants of the Virgin Mary at her coronation and all music and musicians were by tradition considered to be under her protection.

Carvings at Melrose Abbey and Roslin are the earliest, though mute evidence for the bagpipe in Scotland, and given its by then apparently standardised European form as bagpipe with drone (as well seen in an early 15th-century stone frieze in Roslin Chapel), this instrument was adopted from mainstream European culture and not invented or created in Scotland. The carving in stone on Melrose Abbey of a pig playing a bagpipe dates probably from the rebuilding of the Cistercian monastery after its destruction in cross-border raiding from England around 1385.

If we may assume that the pipes were being played in Scotland by the 14th century, we may fairly speculate that they were sharing in the emerging musical heritage of Europe through the burghs and also the royal court. A 15th-century history of Scotland, the 'Scotichronicon', lists music among the accomplishments of James I (r.1424–1437) and describes the King as player of the tabour, the bagpipe, the psaltery, the organ, the flute, the harp, the trumpet and the small shepherd's pipe. If we may doubt whether the King was in reality so multi-talented, at least we gain an insight into the range of performance instruments known in early 15th-century Scotland. The same source describes King James on the night of his murder in the Blackfriars in Perth and again provides an insight into contemporary Scotland's courtly entertainment. The King is said to have '…passed his tyme in reading of romans, in synging and piping, in harping and in other honest solaces of great plesance and disport.'

James I (r.1424–1437). He was a leading poet in his own right, a musician and composer, and was said to "touch the harp like another Orpheus".

Clear evidence for pipes and pipers is otherwise masked by the terminology of the records which generally uses the unspecific 'minstrels' and *joculatores* (later rendered as 'jockies' in vernacular Scots) and it is only with the Exchequer Records for the reign of David II (1329–1371) that we read of payments to pipers; in 1362, the King makes a payment of 40 shillings to pipers, but there are much earlier references, in fact as early as the 13th century and the reign of Alexander III, which tell us that the kings of Scots employed musicians such as harpers. The Treasurer's Accounts which are extant from the later years of James III's reign (1460–1488) and provide a much more detailed record show frequent payments being made to pipers, some of them clearly from England: 'To Inglis pyparis that cam to the castel yet [gate] and playit to the king, 8 pounds 8 shillings.' This was a 'Golden Age' of Renaissance culture, especially in the art of music and in the reign of James IV and the Makars, and Scotland's musical culture stands comparison with the best in Europe. Piping seemed also to have enjoyed a high reputation in England at this time since there were salaried pipers in the English royal court, especially for example in the reigns of Henry V and Henry VI, and some had evidently been sent abroad for training in schools of minstrelsy. Henry VIII (r.1509–1547) has traditionally been regarded as an accomplished musician and composer and an inventory of some 300 musical instruments belonging to the King at the time of his death includes five sets of pipes; one of these is described as 'A Baggepipe with pipes of Ivorie, the bagge covered with purple vellat'.

The Music of the Folk

Though piping was clearly a sort of high art and enjoyed equally by the whole community, it was also true folk music, the separation of 'folk' from 'classical' music, practitioners and performance hardly being applicable in the medieval period and in the sense in which these words are now used. In this period also, the pipes were certainly more widely played throughout Europe than we might imagine today. Artists such as Albrecht Dürer, Breughel and Teniers showed pipers as the normal attendants at all social gatherings in Germany and the Low Countries. It is notable that the pipes are often shown accompanied by the hurdy-gurdy in French, the *vielle à roue*. Looking rather like a lute, this is a string instrument which mimics the pipes; the melody is played by a small keyboard while a wooden wheel turned by a handle acts a continuous bow against the strings and provides a drone.

Latterly, the artists' popular genre paintings often depended on the depiction of a lack of sophistication of peasant society as for example memorably in the work of Pieter Brueghel the Elder, coinciding with the time in the 17th and 18th centuries when the bagpipe was

Piper in an engraving by the German Renaissance artist, Albrecht Dürer, signed and dated 1514. This remarkable portrait may relate to Dürer's own home in Nuremberg which is located on ancient travel and pilgrimage routes and was an important medieval trading centre.

going out of fashion under the influence of new classes of musical instruments with wider ranges and the exploration of scales by composers such as Bach. The pipes existed for the music played on them and the music must have been principally the music of song and dance, forms of entertainment and social interaction enjoyed equally in court, burgh and countryside. The evidence is more fugitive like the instruments themselves, in other words they do not survive, but the bagpipe has always traditionally been given a rural setting. Biblical imagery of the 'Annunciation to the Shepherds' or the 'Adoration of the Shepherds' typically placed the pipes in a rural and a pastoral setting and the metaphor was picked up in a political treatise of 1548, *The Complaynt of Scotland*, where the author tucks an encyclopaedic tour of the Scotland of the mid-16th century between his political arguments. He describes shepherds singing and dancing in an arcadian scene:

> '…ilk ane of them hed ane syndry instrument to play to the laif. The fyrst hed ane drone bag pipe, the nyxt hed ane pipe maid of ane bleddir and of ane reid, the thrid playit on ane trump, the feyrd on ane corne pipe, the fyft playit on ane pipe maid of ane gait horne,

Painted scene in the Playfair Book of Hours, late 15th century; a type of ornate prayer book for private devotions. The biblical episode of the angel bringing news of the Nativity to shepherds gives a bagpipe to one of the shepherds, suggesting that the instrument was customarily associated with the rustic and the pastoral.

the sext playit on ane recordar, the seuint playit on ane fiddil and the last playit on ane quhissil.'

Their excellence was unsurpassed according to the writer of *The Complaynt* and it was said that their exemplar was 'the scheiphyrd Pan that playit to the goddis on his bag pype'. This brief account serves to give us a picture of the range of musical instruments used in popular performance in medieval Scotland and, although there is a stringed instrument, wind predominates.

But the evidence suggests that the art of the bagpipe was as much an urbane and urban art. It may have been simply that the opportunities for employment lay in the burghs and, of the musicians patronised by the Crown, most seemed to have been burgh dwellers. An entry in the Treasurer's Accounts for the year 1581 notes:

'To ane Pyper and ane young boy his Sone that playit in Dalkeyth upon Sonday the XI Day of Junii, fra the Kirk to the Castell befoir his Hienes

XXs.'

The History of the Bagpipe

The association with the supernatural or with evil persisted and became more prevalent from time to time, for example under post-Reformation censorship by the Church and during the 16th- and 17th-century 'witch craze' which swept Europe. The bagpipe was denounced as the Devil's instrument, a motif used sensationally by Robert Burns in 'Tam o' Shanter' where he depicts 'Auld Nick' as piping for the witches' dance. Several of the earlier trials

The Devil playing the pipes for the witches' dance as represented by the artist, John Faed (1819-1902), for an edition of Robert Burns' *Tam o' Shanter* published in 1855.

of those accused of witchcraft induced them to describe occasions in which music and dance played a significant role. At North Berwick in 1659, for example, in the trial of John Douglas and eight women belonging to Tranent, the accused confessed to meeting and dancing with the Devil. Douglas was their piper and the tunes to which they danced were cited as 'Kilt thy coat Maggie and come this way with me' and 'Hulie the bed will fa', and the music for the first of these Devil's melodies was noted in a contemporary manuscript.

There had always been a fashion for adopting and reproducing the literature and music of minstrels, especially that of the troubadour poets and singers of Italy and Provence. Allied to a new fashion for the pastoral and rustic in the 17th and 18th centuries, the piper reappeared in the guise of court musician playing in concerts and operas and *fête champetre* or *fiesta campestre* organised for the Courts of Louis XIV and Louis XV. They began to play a chamber bagpipe which became also the instrument of the French aristocracy in the *Grande Ecurie* and, exquisitely made by professional wind-instrument makers in Paris and elsewhere, used bellows for the supply of air and was called *musette du cour*. Latterly, it had two chanters and a sophisticated form of

Young French piper as wandering minstrel playing for a girl who is also being taught the rudiments of the whistle by his companion. The rustic and arcadian represented a seductive fashion in late 17th and 18th century France.

'shuttle' drone. This type of bagpipe must have been invented as early as the turn of the 17th century since it also appears in the detail of a contemporary painted ceiling now in the National Museums of Scotland. As well as bringing folk music into the new classical domain, since composers such as J S Bach – whose father may well have been a piper – wrote bagpipe music into his compositions, concertos and cantatas were written for the musette by French composers. The Northumbrian small pipes seem to derive closely from the *musette*.

Bach's 'Christmas Oratorio' used bagpipe music and G F Handel also adopted pipe music in dramatic form. Travelling in Italy from 1706, he heard shepherds of the Abruzzi highlands who traditionally came down before Christmas and played bagpipes in the streets of Rome and at shrines. Among the traditional Christmas music which he noted was the so-called 'Pipers' Carol' or *Canzone d'I Zampognari* which he used for part of the Biblical text in his *Messiah*. The bagpipe he heard was almost certainly the remarkable *zampogna* of southern Italy, with two divergent chanters and drones all in the one stock, and used to accompany a bagless pipe or *ciaramella* played by a second musician.

Calabrian shepherd pipers playing during Italian Nativity celebrations, from the engraving of a painting by the Scottish artist Sir David Wilkie, about 1827.

The Music of the Folk

With the expansion of the burghs in late 15th-century Scotland in a period of relative prosperity, they began to employ official pipers or other musicians – the town waits – thus aspiring to emulate the style, revels and ostentation of the courts of king and nobility. Musicians and music at this moment drew the attention of the masterly poet-priest, William Dunbar (c.1460–1514), who as a court poet to James IV addressed 'The Merchantis of Edinburgh' in satirical tone and ridiculed their aspirations:

> 'Your commone menstrallis hes no tone Bot
> 'Now the Day Dawis' and 'Into Joun';
> Cunningar men maun serve Sanct Cloun,
> And nevir to uther craftis clame.
> Think ye not schame,
> To hald sic mowaris on the moyne
> In hurt and sclander of your name!'

This tradition continued unabated and all over Lowland Scotland until the 19th century. It is exemplified and celebrated in stylised form in the remarkable elegy to Habbie Simpson, the town piper of Kilbarchan, by Robert Sempill of Beltrees (c.1595–1665), recalling also a brief list of popular songs and pipe tunes of an early date:

> 'Kilbarchan now may say alas!

'Gentleman-amateur' playing on the bellows-blown Union pipe shown on the frontispiece of John Geoghegan's *Complete Tutor for the Pastoral or New Bagpipe* published about 1745.

For she hath lost her Game and Grace,
Both Trixie and the Maiden Trace;
But what remead?
For no man can supply his place,
Hab Simpson's deid.

Now wha shall play the Day it Dawis
Or Hunt Up, when the cock he crawis?
Or who can for our Kirk town-cause
Stand us in stead?
On Bagpipes now no body blawis
Sen Habbie's dead.'

Burgh Pipers

The evidence for the vigorous tradition of Lowland piping is apparent in burgh records and histories especially from the 16th century, where their appointment, payment, dismissal and generally kenspeckle character is recalled. Sir Walter Scott adds a further significant cultural dimension:

> 'By means of these men, much traditional poetry was preserved which must otherwise have perished. It is certain that, till a very late period, the pipers of whom there was one attached to every Border town of note, and whose office was often hereditary, were the great depositaries of oral and particularly of poetical tradition.'

Pipers and other musicians such as drummers, referred to conventionally in the records as 'swaschers', were employed by the burghs typically to parade the streets at dawn and dusk and to play for the summoning of the indwellers for proclamations and for 'wappenschaws' or musters, what was referred to in the records of Perth as 'the auld loveable use'. An early 19th-century historian described the traditions of the same burgh and coincidentally supplied a list of local favourite pipe-tunes:

'Evening and morning and at other times needful, the pipers march through the town to refresh the lieges with "Broken Bones at Luncarty", "Port Lennox", "Jockie and Sandy", "St Johnstone's Hunt's Up", and the like inspiring strains.'

Pipers also make an appearance in many kirk session records in which they and their kind are frequently censured for profaning the Sabbath. For example, an entry in the Stirling Presbytery Records for 1582 notes the summoning of two pipers, William Wricht and Thomas Edmane, for playing the pipes at Sunday weddings. In *Old Mortality*, Scott with his usual artistry paints an excellent word-picture of the typical town piper in a Lowland burgh. He was said to be endowed with:

'...the Piper's Croft, as it is still called, a field of about an acre in extent, five merks, and a new livery-coat of the town's colours yearly; some hopes of a dollar upon the day of the election of magistrates, providing the Provost were able and willing to afford such a gratuity; and the privilege of paying, at all the respectable houses in the neighbourhood, an annual visit at springtime to rejoice their hearts with his music, to comfort his own

> with their ale and brandy, and to beg from each a modicum of seed-corn.'

A house was often part of the reward of the town pipers, and in Jedburgh for example, the Piper's House can still be seen in Duck Row at the foot of the Canongate, with a stone statuette of a piper set on the crowstepped gable. This was the dwelling of the Hasties, a piping family who held office in the burgh hereditarily from the 15th to the 19th centuries. The list of burghs for which there is evidence about pipers or musicians includes Inverness, Aberdeen, Montrose, Dundee, Perth, St Andrews, Dunfermline, Stirling, Falkirk, Linlithgow, Edinburgh, Haddington, Dumbarton, Glasgow, Lanark, Ayr, Peebles, Selkirk, Hawick, Jedburgh, Dumfries and Berwick.

The town piper of Dalkeith was drawn by the caricaturist, John Kay, in 1789. His etched portrait shows him dressed in his livery coat and playing a set of Lowland bellows pipes, and the figure is subscribed with the legend: 'This represents old Geordy Sime, A Famous Piper in his Time'. His responsibilities and rewards were typical; he received a small salary and a suit of clothes annually in return for playing through the town twice daily, morning and

Geordy Sime, Town Piper of Dalkeith, c.1770, in an etched portrait by the Edinburgh artist and caricaturist, John Kay (1742–1826).

Detail of a scene by the artist, Walter Geikie (1795–1837) showing a seated piper playing on bellows-blown Union or *uilleann* pipes.

evening. It was said that his favourite tunes were 'Go tae Berwick, Johnny' and 'Dalkeith has got a Rare Thing', the last being a favourite of the Duchess of Buccleuch who was customarily greeted with it when arriving or departing the burgh and the neighbouring Dalkeith Palace. The name of the tune was suitably ambivalent and is known also as 'Dunse dings aa", no doubt providing an expedient for earning the rewards of patrons in the Berwickshire burgh of Duns, where their motto or battle-cry proclaimed (as above) that 'Duns beats the lot'!

When the evidence becomes more plentiful in the 18th century, the burgh pipers seem generally to be playing a bellows-blown bagpipe, smaller than the Highland bagpipe as we know it. This 'Lowland' bagpipe had three drones, two tenor and one bass, fixed in a single common stock and was preferred with bellows by which 'cauld wind' (i.e. cold wind) kept the reeds dry and avoided much of the instability and shorter life of mouth-blown reeds. The 'cauld-wind' pipes were energy-saving and labour-saving; it could be played more readily both outside and indoors and was a popular instrument for music and dancing at feasts and festivals, bridals and kirns, the popular feast always with dancing to celebrate the end of harvest. It was widely played in the Lowland and Border country and a surviving relation is the Northumbrian 'Half-Long' bagpipe. As the burgh pipers declined and disappeared in the early 19th century, a change coincidental in time with the Burgh Reform Act of 1833 when, in an increasingly utilitarian age cleansing, lighting, transport and policing had to take precedence over the patronage of simple entertainment, so the instrument itself began to fall out of use. Its role was taken over, on the one hand, by instruments of greater range such as fiddle, concertina and accordion, and, on the other, by the Highland bagpipe which had established its reputation as the marching instrument of military bands.

In case we imagine that Scott embroidered his tale of the toun piper with whimsical detail, an independent account from the factual pen of Robert Chambers in the early 19th century shows how well entrenched and beloved the tradition of the burgh pipers had become, especially as it faded. He was describing the Piper of Peebles, Jamie Ritchie, who had died in 1807 at an advanced age when the author had been five years old and had been living in the family home a few doors from the Piper himself:

Lowland Wedding or the 'Village Dance' after de Witt, late 17th century. The piper is playing for the dancing led by the bridal couple.

The History of the Bagpipe

'Ritchie had been the Piper of Peebles from the year 1741, so that in my childish days he had become a very old man. It was part of his duty to march through the town every evening between nine and ten o'clock, playing on his pipes, as a warning to the inhabitants to go to their beds. He dwelt in a small cottage, where he brought up a family of ten children upon an official salary of a pound a year, the gains he derived from playing at weddings and other festivals, and the little gifts it was customary to give him at the New Year. I remember the old man calling at our house on New Year's Day in the course of the round of visits he then paid the principal citizens, dressed in his official coat of dark red and his cocked hat – rather merry by the time he came to us, in consequence of the drams given him along with the shillings and sixpences. My father had a liking for him, through the sympathy in his nature for everything musical, and one evening he took me with him into Ritchie's cottage, that I might hear some of the old man's tunes. The instrument was not what is called the Great Bagpipe, the bagpipe of the Highlands, blown by the mouth, but the smaller bagpipe inflated by a pair of bellows under the left arm. I suspect that Ritchie had tunes of his own composition, since lost, for there were three called 'Salmon Tails', 'Lyne's Mill Trows' and 'The Black and the Grey' – a racing tune I suspect – which are not to be seen or heard of nowadays.'

The Highland Bagpipe

If the pipes were being played in Scotland by the 14th century, they may have been more or less unknown in the Highlands before about 1400 although Gaelic society had had its own very rich musical tradition. In the present state of knowledge and analysis however, any proposition about the late arrival of the bagpipe in the *Gàidhealtachd* must be little more than guesswork. Early references in Gaelic sources to pipers occur in the first half of the 16th century, such as in the 'Book of the Dean of Lismore' and in a legal document of 1541 by which 'Evano Piper' (presumably *Eòghann*) was witness to a land transaction on behalf of the MacLeods of Dunvegan. The instrument achieved the form recognisable today as the *Piob Mhór* or 'Great Highland Bagpipe' in the late 16th- and 17th centuries, with decorated chanter and powerful drones, the deep bass drone probably predating the tenor drones. When the pipes begin to appear in Gaelic sources such as poetry and song, the immediate impression is of a resounding quality of acoustic power. An eloquent reference in a 17th-century praise-poem by the celebrated Mary MacLeod to her chieftain of MacLeod is not untypical.

The Highland Bagpipe

The piper named was the well-known Patrick Og MacCrimmon:

> *Ach pìob nuallanach mhór*
> *Bheireadh buaidh air gach ceòl*
> *An uair a ghluaiste i le meoir Phàdraig*
> [But the great roaring pipe,
> That would get victory over all other music,
> When it would be stirred by
> Patrick's fingers.]

The coastal fortress of Dunvegan in north-west Skye, the principal residence of the MacLeod chieftains.

Before this, the harp or *clarsach* was the predominant musical instrument of Gaelic society, and the harpers were members of the professional and learned orders which flourished in both Scotland and Ireland until the 17th century. Their decline was swifter in Ireland than in Scotland where one or two of the aristocratic households such as the MacLeans of Duart and the MacLeods of Dunvegan maintained their patronage for the bards and harpers well into the 17th and even 18th centuries. Social and political changes consequent on the break-up of the Lordship of the Isle after 1493 led to the clans fragmenting, struggling to reinstate the Lordship and fighting for territory. More men were brought to the battlefield and there was a simple need for a more carrying sound than could be drawn from the *clarsach*. It must be significant that the first convincing reference to the Highland bagpipe is in the context of war. In *L'Histoire de la Guerre d'Ecosse* published in Paris in 1556, the author, a French military officer probably in the forces of Queen Mary of Guise, describes the massing of the armies before the Battle of Pinkie in 1547: '…the wild [*sauvages*] Scots encouraged themselves to arms by the sound of their bagpipes [*cornemeuses*]', and it is probable that the reference is to the troops brought to the Scottish army by the earl of Argyll.

Neil MacLean, Piper to the Highland Society of London, in a portrait by William Craig, about 1784, playing on a presentation set of pipes.

The History of the Bagpipe

Although the courts of the chieftains were losing some of their former glory enjoyed under the earlier Lordship of the Isles, the piper seemed to slip naturally into the warrior-hero culture of Gaelic Scotland. At first he appeared to be despised and there are Gaelic songs of dispraise of this incomer and upstart. The sound of the pipes was compared variously to pigs, ducks and geese, and a typically crushing bardic line was: 'better used as a rattle for

'Highland Piper', fallen on hard times and begging in the street with a lad or 'gillie', possibly in the Edinburgh area in the 1830s. Coloured etching by Walter Geikie.

scaring horses out of a hayfield than for inciting a host'. The earliest of these denunciations was by the late 16th-century bard, Niall Mór MacMhuirich, who composed a highly satirical 'History of the Pipes from the Beginning of Time' *Seanchas na Pìoba o Thùs*. He starts with an 'overblown pig's bladder' and sustains the parody by referring to presumably well-known pipers in this vein, and closes after eleven stanzas with *pìob ghleadhair*… 'the noisy, clashing pipes, musical sweetheart for the ear of the Black Fiend'. This drew a response in praise of the pipes and a tradition of praise, or *moladh*, and dispraise, or *di-moladh*, developed which continued as a suitable arena for bardic context well into the 18th century. Of course there were always both good and bad performers and the standards were high, but the tone of hyperbole in these Gaelic songs suggests that satire was more important than assertion.

There was clearly a role for an imported musical instrument; the patronage of the chieftains still earned the poets' and musicians' extravagant praise in eulogy and elegy, and the pipes were capable of supplying this in abundance. Mary MacLeod (c.1615–1707) again captures the essence of this traditional culture of performance and remuneration in her clan panegyric giving recognition to the chieftain's Hall at Dunvegan as a vital epicentre of Gaelic culture:

> *Gu àros nach crìon*
> *Am bi gàirich nam pìob*
> 'To the dwelling that is not mean
> Where the roar of the pipes will be,
> And again the sound of the harps,
> With the glint of silver cups,
> Making wine flow free
> And pouring into the handiwork
> of the goldsmith.'

The bagpipe overtook the harp in popularity and prestige as the musical instrument of Gaelic society and assumed a traditional role in Gaelic culture. In its own unique idiom which is this form of classical music known as *ceòl mór* or 'pibroch', it inherited and to some extent complemented the bardic tradition of *brosnachadh* – encouragement and incitement – the praise of warriors and chieftains and the lament for their passing. The pipes were played in the Great Hall of the chieftain to mark important occasions for kin and clan, and also naturally for dancing and entertainment. Pipers would customarily be rewarded with a croft or farm to be occupied rent-free in return for the service of playing the pipes at the chieftain's behest. In several instances, the piper's croft became a centre of musical excellence and pipers were sent to learn their art to perfection with the acknowledged masters. Tradition in Gaelic records the use of the term *oil-thaigh* or 'university' for these and supplies some indication of the status and nature of such centres. A seemingly modest dwelling at Peingown in the north end of Skye might hold much greater significance than what met the eye. In 1772 the travel-writer, Thomas Pennant, described the house of the MacArthur piper to the MacDonald of Sleat clan chieftain:

'Take a repast at the house of Sir Alexander MacDonald's piper, who, according to antient custom, by virtue of his office, holds his lands free. His dwelling, like many others in this country, consists of several apartments: the first for his cattle during winter, the second is his hall, the third for the reception of strangers, and the fourth for the lodging of his family, all the rooms within one another...The owner was quite master of his instrument, and treated us with several tunes. In feudal times the MacDonalds had in this island a college of pipers, and the MacLeods had the like.'

Even in the clan territory of Clan Donald, bardic opinion was unanimous that the MacCrimmons of Skye and Glenelg were pre-eminent: '*Air na pìobairean uile, b'e Mac Cruimein an Rìgh*' ('Of all pipers, MacCrimmon was king') it was said, and this perceived pre-eminence of the MacCrimmons as pipers through successive generations to the MacLeods of Dunvegan was maintained and has survived in the art of the Highland bagpipe to this day. Other family dynasties of pipers emerged besides the MacCrimmons of Harris and Skye, such as the MacKays of Gairloch and Raasay, the MacArthurs in Skye, the Rankins in Mull, the MacGregors of Glenlyon, the MacIntyres of Rannoch, and the Cummings of Badenoch and Strathspey, the successive generations of whom performed the duties of official piper for their clan chieftain patrons through hundreds of years and who sustained and generated the music of the bagpipe until the collapse of the society which nurtured them in the wake of the Jacobite wars of the 18th century.

On 15th November 1746, James Reid, Piper, was executed at York as a rebel. In his trial which was reported in the *Scots Magazine* it was alleged in his defence that he had not carried arms, but the Court observed that a Highland regiment never

Peter Henderson (1851–1903), bagpipe maker of renown, piper and music collector and publisher. He founded his business in Glasgow in 1868, typically taking over the premises of another pipemaker, collector and publisher, Donald Macphee.

marched without a piper and therefore that his bagpipe in the eyes of the law was an instrument of war. After this debacle, the Highland bagpipe survived by virtue of the growth of empire and standing armies rather than by virtue at the time of its art, and these influences also standardised the instrument and styles of playing. Military performance demanded uniformity, discipline and unison, and the Highland piper as soloist and in pipe bands followed the British Army round the world from the late 18th century. The memorials to this history are seen in the continuing tradition of military pipe bands in the Middle East, Pakistan, India and Nepal where, for example, the Gurkha soldiers are particularly enthusiastic exponents of the Highland bagpipe, and in Common-wealth and Dominion countries such as Canada and Australia whose own pipers and pipe bands have now challenged the leadership of Scotland's own military and civilian bands. Many of the great pipe tunes are recollections of theatres of war and feats of arms: 'The Barren Rocks of Aden' (c.1844), 'The 79th Farewell to Gibraltar' (c.1848), 'The Siege of Delhi', 'The 25th KOSB's Farewell to Meerut' (the site of a large military cantonment and the outbreak of the Indian Mutiny in 1857), 'The 93rd at Modder River' (c.1899), and so on.

Siubhal

This term in Scottish Gaelic means 'journey' or 'march' and can be taken to symbolise the survival and versatility of the bagpipe in Scotland. It is also used specifically in 'pibroch' as the term for the movement that is a key variation on the melody. On the one hand therefore it speaks expressively of pipe music and on the other may be taken as symbolic of a remarkable tradition. The 'Pibroch of Donald Dubh' is a well-known and popular brisk marching tune today and reflects the survival and adaptability that we sense in this history. It is also an early 15th-century pibroch-song and one of the oldest known of vernacular Gaelic songs still popular today. In the reiterative style of the lyrics we hear the phrasing of bagpipe music, and the resounding words of summons belong typically to the praise poetry of warriors and wars in which the Highland bagpipe seemed to flourish:

Pìob agus bratach air faich Ionarlòchaidh
['The bagpipe and the standard on the parade-field of Inverlochy']

If the bagpipe is not so closely associated with wars and warfare today, its survival in Scotland

Detail from 'Coronach in the Backwoods' by George W Simson, 1859. The pioneer settler in North America plays a lament while his wife weeps on receiving news from home – a strong but sentimentalised image of the Highland Clearances.

owed much to the army where the instrument evolved its distinctive music of marches and quicksteps which at the same time developed a form of 'exhibition' music for competition. Under a new patronage of the officer-class of the British army and of contemporary improving clubs and societies, competition became the life-blood of the art. The Highland Society of London, founded in 1778, inaugurated a piping competition at the Cattle Tryst at Falkirk in October 1781 and in essence such competitions continue to this day. Initially these competitions were for 'pibroch' playing but soon came to include the march, strathspey and reel, pre-existing and traditional tune-types in many instances but in slower tempo and with elaborate gracenoting. In many cases old melodies were adopted and extended so that, for example, the ribald old melody of 'Stumpie' traditionally played at bridals evolved into a six-part march tune, 'Highland Wedding'. Typical of the compositions in a similar style which then emerged are 'The Balmoral Highlanders' by Queen Victoria's Piper, Angus Mackay, and 'The Atholl High-landers March to Loch Katrine' of 1859.

These and other tunes, with their note of the romance of the Highland warrior of old, become

Piper George Clark, 71st Highlanders (later the Highland Light Infantry), who although wounded continued to play his pipes at the Battle of Vimiera in Portugal in 1808. He received a set of silver-mounted pipes from the Caledonian Society of London for his courage.

a metaphor for how the pipes have evolved in Scotland over the last 200 years. They would usually be heard played by virtuoso pipers on the battlefield of Highland Games competition but recently standards of judging and competitions have been questioned for inhibiting musical expression and forcing the music into a straitjacket which forbade interpretation or innovation. But a prevailing concept of 'world music' and its search for something different has now recognised a high value in Scottish music, and 'new-wave folk' of the last two decades has embraced the *ceilidh* tradition and the high quality and expertise of today's pipers. This is without doubt a dynamic culture and a self-conscious and a confident one. Whereas piping both in Scotland and in Europe as a whole had been characterised, as we have seen, by an almost bewildering variety of music and playing styles, and of the instrument itself, the longer term impression had been one of crisis, decline and disappearance. This is no longer the case; in Scotland, the earlier familiarity with primitive hornpipe, the Lowland bellows pipe, the small pipe, pastoral pipe and Great Highland pipe has again entered our consciousness and culture.

Further Reading

Allain, Emile, *Traité Elémentaire destiné aux Sonneurs de Biniou*, Editions BAS, 1965, 1977

Baines, Anthony, *Bagpipes*, Occasional Papers on Technology 9, Pitt Rivers Museum University of Oxford, revised edition 1973

Buchan, David, *The Ballad and the Folk*, London 1972, new edition 1997

Campbell, Archibald, *The Kilberry Book of Ceòl Mór*, Aird & Coghill Glasgow, second edition 1953

Campsie, Alistair Keith, *The MacCrimmon Legend – The Madness of Angus Mackay*, Canongate Edinburgh, 1980

Cannon, Roderick D, *A Bibliography of Bagpipe Music*, John Donald Edinburgh, 1980

Cannon, Roderick D, ed., *Joseph MacDonald's Compleat Theory of the Scots Highland Bagpipe* (c.1760), The Piobaireachd Society, 1994

Cannon, Roderick D, *The Highland Bagpipe and its Music*, John Donald Edinburgh, 1988

Castel, Yves, *Le Biniou et la Bombarde en couple*, Editions Breizh Hor Bro, 1980

Cheape, Hugh, 'The Bagadoù of Brittany', in *The International Piper* Volume 2 Part 5 (1979), 5–6

Cheape, Hugh, 'The Piper to the Laird of Grant', in *Proceedings of the Society of Antiquaries of Scotland* Volume 125 (1995), 1163–1173

Collinson, Francis, *The Bagpipe – The history of a musical instrument*, Routledge & Kegan Paul London, 1975

Collinson, Francis, *The Traditional and National Music of Scotland*, Routledge & Kegan Paul London, 1966

Dalyell, John G, *Musical Memoirs of Scotland, with Historical Annotations*, T G Stevenson Edinburgh, 1849

Farmer, Henry G, *A History of Music in Scotland*, Hinrichsen London, 1947

Johnson, David, *Music and Society in Lowland Scotland in the Eighteenth Century*, Oxford University Press, 1972

Johnson, James, *The Scots Musical Museum*, new edition with notes by William Stenhouse and David Laing, Edinburgh, 1853, Scolar Press, 1991

MacKenzie, John, *The Beauties of Gaelic Poetry*, Norman MacLeod Edinburgh, 1904

MacNeill, Seumas, and Richardson, Frank, *Piobaireachd and its Interpretation: Classical Music of the Highland Bagpipe*, John Donald Edinburgh, 1987

Macpherson, Angus, *A Highlander Looks Back*, Oban, 1955

Matheson, William, *The Blind Harper. The Songs of Roderick Morison and his Music*, Scottish Gaelic Texts Society Edinburgh, 1970

Melville-Mason, G, *An Exhibition of European Musical Instruments*, Galpin Society Edinburgh, 1968

Purser, John, *Scotland's Music*, Mainstream Edinburgh, 1992

Scott, Walter, *Old Mortality*, Border Edition Edinburgh & London, 1893

Stewart, A M, ed., *The Complaynt of Scotland by Mr Robert Wedderburn*, The Scottish Texts Society Edinburgh, 1979

Acknowledgements

I would like to thank Roderick Cannon and Allan MacDonald for discussing the topic of piping with me on innumerable occasions and for reading through this book in draft. Any errors and ambiguities remain to be explained solely by the author. I would also like to thank the Director and Trustees of the National Museums of Scotland for their encouragement and Appletree Press for enthusiastic help with the book.

Page 4 © National Museums of Scotland, first published Kenneth MacLeay Highlanders of Scotland

Page 6 © National Museums of Scotland OD69

Page 13 © National Museums of Scotland LT6

Page 18 (first published in Anthony Baines, *Bagpipes* Occasional Papers on Technology 9, Pitt Rivers Museum, University of Oxford, revised edition 1973)

Page 20 © National Museum of Scotland 1947. 122 (Duncan Fraser Collection)

Page 22 © National Museums of Scotland, first published Henry Blackburn and Randolph Caldecott *Breton Folk, An artistic tour of*

Acknowledgements

Brittany London 1880

Page 24 © National Museums of Scotland, first published R R Mclan and James Logan, *The Clans of the Scottish Highlands* London 1847

Page 29 © National Museums of Scotland

Page 31 © National Museums of Scotland

Page 34 © National Museums of Scotland KL131

Page 38 © National Museums of Scotland, first published J J Jusserand, *English Wayfaring Life in the Middle Ages* London 1888

Page 40 © National Museums of Scotland

Page 44 © National Museums of Scotland, first published C N MacIntyre North, *The Book of the Club of True Highlanders* London 1881

Page 46 © National Museums of Scotland, first published Matthew Guthrie *Les Antiquités de Russie* St Petersbourg 1795

Page 52 © Scottish National Portrait Gallery, Edinburgh

Page 56 © National Museums of Scotland

Page 58 © Victoria and Albert Picture Library

Page 60 © National Museums of Scotland

Page 62 © National Museums of Scotland

Page 64 © National Museums of Scotland

Page 66 © National Museums of Scotland 1947. 129 (Duncan Fraser Collection)

Page 71 © National Museums of Scotland, first published, John Kay, *A Series of Original Portraits and Caricature Etchings* Edinburgh 1842

Page 72 © National Museums of Scotland, first published, *Etchings Illustrative of Scottish Character and Scenery* Edinburgh c. 1842

Page 75 © National Museums of Scotland OD6

Page 79 © National Museums of Scotland

Page 81 © National Museums of Scotland

Page 82 © National Museums of Scotland, *Etchings Illustrative of Scottish Character and Scenery* Edinburgh c. 1842 (Bute Collection)

Page 87 © National Museums of Scotland

Page 90 © National Museums of Scotland OD8

Page 92 © National Museums of Scotland